◤ SCHOLASTIC

Alpha Tales

New York • Toronto • London • Auckland • Sydney
Mexico City • New Delhi • Hong Kong • Buenos Aires

Cover designed by Michelle H. Kim

ISBN: 978-1-338-11697-7

1 2 3 4 5 6 7 8 9 10   157   22 21 20 19 18 17 16

Contents

Welcome to

Alpha Tales

This cheerful collection of stories is here to help you help your child build key alphabet skills that will lay the foundation for literacy success and a lifelong love of reading!

Two powerful predictors of literacy success are alphabet recognition (knowing the names of letters and the sounds they represent) and phonemic awareness (understanding that a word is made up of a series of discrete sounds). A mastery of these early skills opens the gate to reading fluency. Without a thorough knowledge of letters and an understanding that words are made up of sounds, children cannot learn to read.

Throughout a child's preschool years, letters are learned by singing the rhythmic ABC song, being exposed to alphabet books, watching educational programs, and having family members identify letters on signs as well as in the child's name. Children eagerly engage in these activities—all with the understanding that this set of 26 remarkable letters holds the key to written language.

Because of this early exposure to the alphabet, many children enter school already able to say their ABCs. However, being able to say the names of letters is not the same as "knowing" the letters. In order to learn to read, children must be able to identify the printed forms of all the letters—in and out of sequence—and learn the most frequent sound attached to each one.

The speed, or *automaticity*, with which children recognize the letters is also important. For automaticity to take place, children must "over-learn" the letters of the alphabet via lots of varied practice. Research shows that children who can recognize letters with accuracy and speed are on track to become confident, agile readers. But where do parents find the tools to help their children develop these essential skills?

The answer is *Alpha Tales!* This lively collection is the perfect way to teach all the critical aspects of alphabet recognition. The stories will help your child . . .

- identify each letter of the alphabet.

- associate each letter with a sound.

- develop phonemic awareness skills.

- build oral language skills.

- expand vocabulary and word knowledge.

- boost early comprehension skills.

While most alphabet books allow a page or two for each letter, *Alpha Tales* devotes an entire story to each, enabling you to immerse your child in words that begin with that target letter. Research shows that as children learn letters, they frequently become interested in learning more about them—including their sounds and how to use them to write words. The *Alpha Tales* stories offer a language-rich context for these exciting explorations.

Teaching the common, one-to-one correspondence of a letter to a sound helps children develop a deep understanding of the alphabetic principle. For some children, this is an easy-to-achieve "Aha" moment. Reading quickly becomes a fun puzzle in which they graft a sound onto a letter (or letter cluster), then blend many sounds together to read words. For other children, however, the process requires extra practice and patience. These children need additional opportunities to hear and say the sounds as well as to write and play with the letters. *Alpha Tales* is the ideal tool to help them to do just that!

Some additional ideas for at-home instruction include the following:

Letter List: Select a letter and work with your child to brainstorm a long list of words that begin with it. Can you think of ten or more?

Letter Clap: Pick a letter. Then read an *Alpha Tales* story aloud, inviting your child to clap each time a word is read that begins with that letter.

Letter Collage: Use magazines and/or pictures downloaded from the internet to craft a lively collage of items that begin with a target letter.

Edible Letter: Encourage your child to build his or her favorite letter (or letters) out of cereal or pasta pieces.

Letter Guess: Select a letter and provide your child with a quick clue to its identity, such as, *It is the last letter of the alphabet and it begins the word* zoo. Can he or she guess it?

Letter Hunt: Challenge your child to look around the room and find as many items as he or she can that begin with a target letter.

Letter Match: Write upper- and lowercase letters from A to Z on separate index cards. Then use them to play matching games.

Letter Tongue Twister: Make up a silly tongue twister that celebrates a target letter such as: *Abby the alligator absolutely adores awesome apples!* Can your child say it five times fast?

Letter Bag: Place the letters A to Z in a paper bag. Invite your child to choose one and provide clues to help *you* guess it.

Read, Read, Read: Read and reread *Alpha Tales* as well as a host of other ABC books. There is no such thing as too much reading!

Remember, a child's long educational journey begins with a simple tune—"A, B, C, D, E, F, G . . . Now I know my ABCs!" Since English is an alphabetic language, it makes sense to start our youngest learners on the path to mastering this special set of squiggles and lines that, when combined, create something spectacular—printed words! As you use *Alpha Tales* to teach your child the letters of the alphabet and their corresponding sounds, be sure to enjoy and savor the stories. Share your own enthusiasm for our sometimes complex, always magical, written language. Introducing your child to the joys of literacy is one of the most important things you can do as a caregiver.

Happy reading!

Wiley Blevins
Ed.M., Harvard University

The Adventures of Abby Alligator

By Maria Fleming
Illustrated by Matt Phillips

Here are some quick and fun ways to use this story to help children build important alphabet recognition skills.

- Ask children to find big A and small a at the top of the previous page. Review the long A/a and short A/a sounds with children. Can they find three words in the title that begin with the letter A/a? Read the title aloud, emphasizing the A/a sound as appropriate.

- Ask children to point out words they hear or see that begin with A/a. Explain that the story you are about to read includes many more words that begin with the letter A/a. Can they help you find them?

- Read the story aloud once for pleasure and enjoy together the whimsical illustrations. Then reread the story, emphasizing the initial A/a sound in the appropriate words. Ask children to listen closely for and identify all the words that start with A/a. Point out these words in the text, and make a list of them.

- Write each of the words from your list on an unlined index card. Read each word on the cards aloud with children. On another reading of the story, children can match the words on the index cards with the words in the story.

- Read aloud the cheer on page 24 several times, with lots of energy and enthusiasm. Invite children to join you in reciting the cheer when they feel ready. Encourage them to find any new A/a words in the cheer. Again, add these words to your list.

- Don't let your exploration of the letter A/a end with the story! Display your list of words in a place where children can easily see it. During the rest of the day or week, children can add new A/a words that they encounter in other books, on signs, on food labels, and so on.

Abby Alligator is ready to work.
What will Abby do?

Abby wants to be an acrobat.

But she's afraid of falling.

Abby wants to be an artist.
But she can only paint apples.

Abby wants to be an animal doctor.
But she's allergic to aardvarks.

Abby wants to be an astronaut.

But she meets an angry alien.

Abby wants to be an actor.

But she is awful.

Abby can't think of any other jobs.

Then Abby has an AMAZING idea.
"I'll be an author!" Abby says.

Abby Alligator writes all about her
adventures as an acrobat, an artist,
an animal doctor, an astronaut,
and an actor.

Being an author is AWESOME!

Aa Cheer

A is for alligator and acorns on trees.

A is for "Ah-choo!" when you sneeze.

A is for apples baked in a pie.

A is for airplane up in the sky.

Hooray for A, big and small—

the most awesome, amazing letter of all!

Bubble Bear

By Maxwell Higgins

Illustrated by Maxie Chambliss

Reading Tips

Here are some quick and fun ways to use this story to help children build important alphabet recognition skills.

- Ask children to find big B and small b at the top of the previous page. Review the B/b sound with children. Can they find two words in the title that begin with the letter B/b? Read the title aloud, emphasizing the B/b sound as appropriate.

- Ask children to point out words they hear or see that begin with B/b. Explain that the story you are about to read includes many more words that begin with the letter B/b. Can they help you find them?

- Read the story aloud once for pleasure and enjoy together the whimsical illustrations. Then reread the story, emphasizing the initial B/b sound in the appropriate words. Ask children to listen closely for and identify all the words that start with B/b. Point out these words in the text, and make a list of them.

- Write each of the words from your list on an unlined index card. Read each word on the cards aloud with children. On another reading of the story, children can match the words on the index cards with the words in the story.

- Read aloud the cheer on page 40 several times, with lots of energy and enthusiasm. Invite children to join you in reciting the cheer when they feel ready. Encourage them to find any new B/b words in the cheer. Again, add these words to your list.

- Don't let your exploration of the letter B/b end with the story! Display your list of words in a place where children can easily see it. During the rest of the day or week, children can add new B/b words that they encounter in other books, on signs, on food labels, and so on.

Bear was the best bubble blower
on his block. Bear could blow
great big bubbles.

Bear could blow itsy-bitsy bubbles.

Bear could even blow a bubble beard!

Bear could blow lots of bubble shapes, too.

Bear could blow a bubble bell

and a bubble birthday cake

and a bubble bunny

and, of course, a bubble bear!

One day, Badger saw Bear blowing bubbles.
Badger was a bully.
Everyone on the block was afraid of her.

"Only babies blow bubbles," Badger told Bear.
But Bear kept right on blowing.
He blew and blew until he had blown…

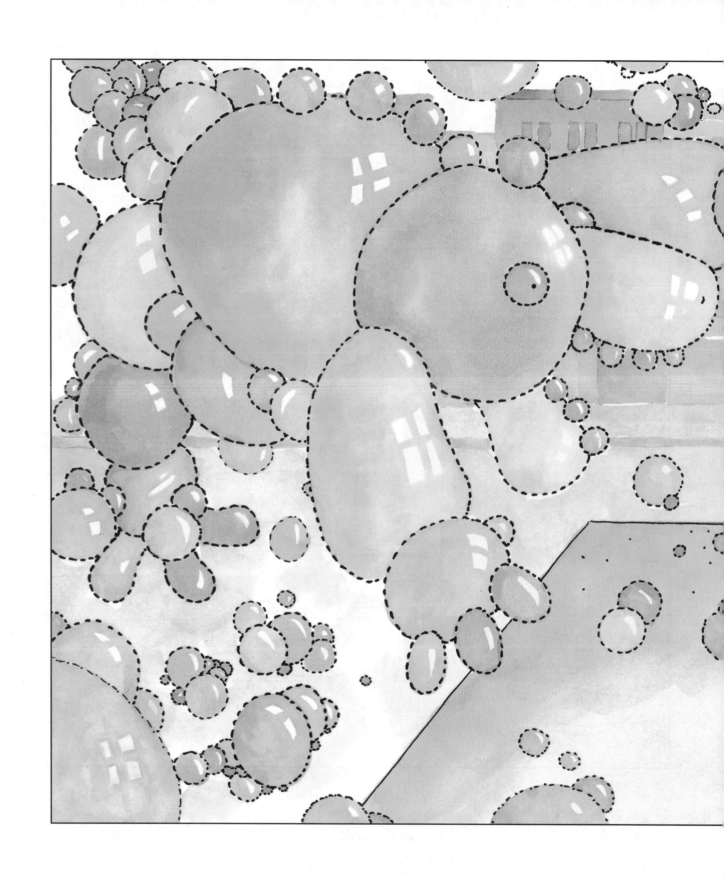

...a great big bubble beast!

"Ahhhhh!" yelled Badger.
She ran behind a bush.

"Only babies are afraid of bubbles!"
Bear told Badger.

"Bear, I am sorry I called you a baby,"
said Badger. "Will you show me how
you blow such beautiful bubbles?"

So Bear showed Badger how to blow big bubbles and itsy-bitsy bubbles. He showed her how to blow a bubble beard, a bubble bell, and a bubble birthday cake.

He showed her how to blow a bubble
bunny, a bubble bear, and a bubble badger.
And Bear even showed Badger how to blow
a great big bubble beast!

Bb Cheer

B is for bear, bubbles, and boat.

B is for buttons on your coat.

B is for bicycle, bunny, and bat.

B is for bee—imagine that!

Hooray for B, big and small—

The best, most beautiful letter of all!

AlphaTales

Copycats

BY MARIA FLEMING
ILLUSTRATED BY HANS WILHELM

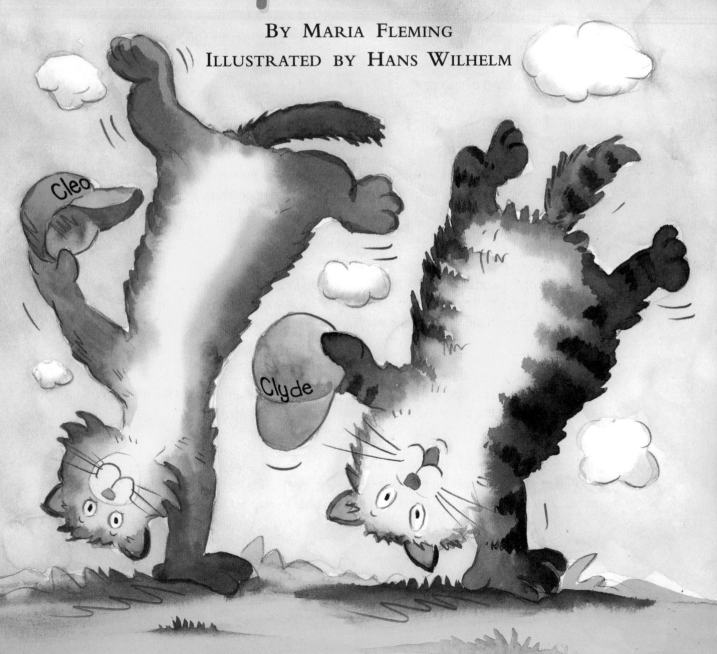

Reading Tips

Here are some quick and fun ways to use this story to help children build important alphabet recognition skills.

- Ask children to find big C and small c at the top of the previous page. Review the C/c sound with children. Can they find a word on the cover that begins with the letter C/c? Read the title aloud, emphasizing the C/c sound as appropriate.

- Ask children to point out words they hear or see that begin with C/c. Explain that the story you are about to read includes many more words that begin with the letter C/c. Can they help you find them?

- Read the story aloud once for pleasure and enjoy together the whimsical illustrations. Then reread the story, emphasizing the initial C/c sound in the appropriate words. Ask children to listen closely for and identify all the words that start with C/c. Point out these words in the text, and make a list of them.

- Write each of the words from your list on an unlined index card. Read each word on the cards aloud with children. On another reading of the story, children can match the words on the index cards with the words in the story.

- Read aloud the cheer on page 56 several times, with lots of energy and enthusiasm. Invite children to join you in reciting the cheer when they feel ready. Encourage them to find any new C/c words in the cheer. Again, add these words to your list.

- Read aloud the cheer on page 16 several times, with lots of energy and enthusiasm. Invite children to join you in reciting the cheer when they feel ready. Encourage them to find any new C/c words in the cheer. Again, add these words to your list.

Clyde and Cleo are cats—copycats!
"I bet you can't do what I can do,"
says Clyde.
"I can too!" says Cleo.

"I can do a cartwheel," says Clyde.
"Can you?"
"I can too!" says Cleo.

"I can ride a camel," says Cleo.
"Can you?"
"I can too!" says Clyde.

"I can bake a coconut cake,"
says Clyde. "Can you?"

"I can too!" says Cleo.

"I can build a castle," says Cleo.
"Can you?"

"I can too!" says Clyde.

"I can grow carrots, corn, and cabbages," says Clyde. "Can you?"

"I can too!" says Cleo.

"I can carry a cup of cocoa
on my head," says Cleo.
"Can you?"

"I can too!" says Clyde.
"Look out for the car!" yells Cleo.

Clyde crashes into Cleo.
The cups crash to the ground.

Clyde looks at Cleo. Cleo looks at Clyde.
They are both covered in cocoa.
"I can stop being a copycat,"
says Clyde. "Can you?"
"I can too," says Cleo.

Cc Cheer

C is for cat, C is for cap.

C is for carrot, crayon, and clap.

C is for camel, cow, cup, and car.

C is cookies in a cookie jar.

Hooray for C, big and small—

the coolest, craziest letter of all!

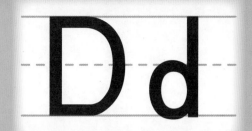

Detective Dog and the Disappearing Doughnuts

BY VALERIE GARFIELD
ILLUSTRATED BY PAUL HARVEY

Reading Tips

Here are some quick and fun ways to use this story to help children build important alphabet recognition skills.

- Ask children to find big D and small d at the top of the previous page. Review the D/d sound with children. Can they find four words in the title that begin with the letter D/d? Read the title aloud, emphasizing the D/d sound as appropriate.

- Ask children to point out words they hear or see that begin with D/d. Explain that the story you are about to read includes many more words that begin with the letter D/d. Can they help you find them?

- Read the story aloud once for pleasure and enjoy together the whimsical illustrations. Then reread the story, emphasizing the initial D/d sound in the appropriate words. Ask children to listen closely for and identify all the words that start with D/d. Point out these words in the text, and make a list of them.

- Write each of the words from your list on an unlined index card. Read each word on the cards aloud with children. On another reading of the story, children can match the words on the index cards with the words in the story.

- Read aloud the cheer on page 72 several times, with lots of energy and enthusiasm. Invite children to join you in reciting the cheer when they feel ready. Encourage them to find any new D/d words in the cheer. Again, add these words to your list.

- Don't let your exploration of the letter D/d end with the story! Display your list of words in a place where children can easily see it. During the rest of the day or week, children can add new D/d words that they encounter in other books, on signs, on food labels, and so on.

Detective Dog went to Dave's Diner
every day for dinner.

For dessert, Detective Dog
always ordered a doughnut.
Detective Dog LOVED doughnuts.

One day after dinner, Detective Dog
said to Dave, "Today is my birthday.
I think I will have TWO doughnuts
for dessert to celebrate."
"On the double, Detective," said Dave.

"Oh, dear!" Dave cried.
"The doughnuts have disappeared!"
"Doggone it!" said Detective Dog.
"I have some detecting to do!"

Suddenly, Detective Dog noticed something
near the door. Powdered sugar!
"If I follow this trail of doughnut dust,
I bet I'll find the thief!" she said.

Detective Dog followed the trail
of doughnut dust downtown.

She followed it past Drake's Drugstore
and the department store.

The trail lead right into Debbie's Deli.
"The doughnut-napper must be in here!"
said Detective Dog.

Detective Dog turned the doorknob.
She stepped inside the deli.
It was completely dark.

Suddenly, the light flashed on.
"SURPRISE!" yelled Detective Dog's friends.

"Hot diggity dog!" said the detective.
"It's a birthday party!"

Dave told Detective Dog that he only
pretended the doughnuts had disappeared.
Dave made the trail of doughnut dust
to lead the detective to the party.

Detective Dog was delighted with the party.
There were dazzling decorations and
dandy gifts. And best of all, there were
dozens and dozens of delicious doughnuts!

Dd Cheer

D is for dog and doughnut, too.

D is for dolphin in the ocean blue.

D is for doll, doctor, and door.

D is for duck and dinosaur.

Hooray for D, big and small—

the most dazzling, delightful letter of all!

AlphaTales

Ee

The Enormous Elephant Show

BY LIZA CHARLESWORTH

ILLUSTRATED BY NADINE BERNARD WESTCOTT

Reading Tips

Here are some quick and fun ways to use this story to help children build important alphabet recognition skills.

- Ask children to find big E and small e at the top of the previous page. Review the long E/e and short E/e sounds with children. Can they find two words in the title that begin with the letter E/e? Read the title aloud, emphasizing the E/e sound as appropriate.

- Ask children to point out words they hear or see that begin with D/d. Explain that the story you are about to read includes many more words that begin with the letter D/d. Can they help you find them?

- Read the story aloud once for pleasure and enjoy together the whimsical illustrations. Then reread the story, emphasizing the initial E/e sound in the appropriate words. Ask children to listen closely for and identify all the words that start with E/e. Point out these words in the text, and make a list of them.

- Write each of the words from your list on an unlined index card. Read each word on the cards aloud with children. On another reading of the story, children can match the words on the index cards with the words in the story.

- Read aloud the cheer on page 88 several times, with lots of energy and enthusiasm. Invite children to join you in reciting the cheer when they feel ready. Encourage them to find any new E/e words in the cheer. Again, add these words to your list.

- Don't let your exploration of the letter E/e end with the story! Display your list of words in a place where children can easily see it. During the rest of the day or week, children can add new E/e words that they encounter in other books, on signs, on food labels, and so on.

Elvin the Elephant is waiting backstage.
To start his show, just turn the page.

Elvin the Elephant makes an E out of eels!

Elvin the Elephant tosses eggplants to seals!

Elvin the Elephant does excellent dives!

Elvin the Elephant bakes elderberry pies!

Elvin the Elephant pulls an elk from a hat!

Elvin the Elephant sends e-mail to his cat!

Elvin the Elephant models elegant clothes!

Elvin the Elephant skates with eggs on his toes!

Elvin the Elephant climbs evergreen trees!

Elvin the Elephant eats a mountain of peas!

Elvin the Elephant exercises with a cow!

Elvin the Elephant takes an enormous bow!

Ee Cheer

E is for elephant, E is for ear.

E is for elk, a kind of deer.

E is for egg, elbow, and eye.

E is for eagle that soars through the sky.

Hooray for E, big and small—

the most excellent, exciting letter of all!

Fifi Ferret's Flute

BY SAMANTHA BERGER

ILLUSTRATED BY ANNE KENNEDY

Here are some quick and fun ways to use this story to help children build important alphabet recognition skills.

- Ask children to find big F and small f at the top of the previous page. Review the F/f sound with children. Can they find three words in the title that begin with the letter F/f? Read the title aloud, emphasizing the F/f sound as appropriate.

- Ask children to point out words they hear or see that begin with F/f. Explain that the story you are about to read includes many more words that begin with the letter F/f. Can they help you find them?

- Read the story aloud once for pleasure and enjoy together the whimsical illustrations. Then reread the story, emphasizing the initial F/f sound in the appropriate words. Ask children to listen closely for and identify all the words that start with F/f. Point out these words in the text, and make a list of them.

- Write each of the words from your list on an unlined index card. Read each word on the cards aloud with children. On another reading of the story, children can match the words on the index cards with the words in the story.

- Read aloud the cheer on page 104 several times, with lots of energy and enthusiasm. Invite children to join you in reciting the cheer when they feel ready. Encourage them to find any new F/f words in the cheer. Again, add these words to your list.

- Don't let your exploration of the letter F/f end with the story! Display your list of words in a place where children can easily see it. During the rest of the day or week, children can add new F/f words that they encounter in other books, on signs, on food labels, and so on.

When Fifi Ferret was five years old,
her father gave her a flute.

Fifi Ferret loved her flute...

She played it for her family.

She played it in the forest.

She played it in fields of flowers.

One day, Fifi was playing her flute by the river.
Suddenly, the flute fell from Fifi's hands!

The flute floated far, far away.
Fifi ran after it.

The flute floated past Frog,
who was catching flies.
"Follow that flute!" yelled Fifi.

The flute floated past Fawn,
who was nibbling ferns.
"Follow that flute!" yelled Fifi and Frog.

The flute floated past Fox,
who was eating figs.
"Follow that flute!" yelled Fifi, Frog, and Fawn.

The flute floated past Flamingo,
who was fluffing her feathers.
"Follow that flute!" yelled Fifi, Frog,
Fawn, and Fox.

Fifi, Frog, Fawn, Fox, and Flamingo ran fast.
But the flute floated faster.
"Oh no! It's floating toward the falls!" Fifi cried.
Fifi feared her flute would be lost forever.

All of a sudden,
Fish leapt from the water.

She grabbed the flute right before it fell down the falls!

Fifi was so happy to have her flute back!

But Fifi was even happier to have such fabulous friends.

Ff Cheer

F is for ferret, F is for flute.

F is for flower, feather, and fruit.

F is for frog, friend, and French fries.

F is for fox and fireflies.

Hooray for F, big and small—

the most fantastic, fabulous letter of all!

Gorilla, Be Good!

By Maria Fleming

Illustrated by Matt Phillips

Reading Tips

Here are some quick and fun ways to use this story to help children build important alphabet recognition skills.

- Ask children to find big G and small g at the top of the previous page. Review the G/g sound with children. Can they find two words in the title that begin with the letter G/g? Read the title aloud, emphasizing the G/g sound as appropriate.

- Ask children to point out words they hear or see that begin with G/g. Explain that the story you are about to read includes many more words that begin with the letter G/g. Can they help you find them?

- Read the story aloud once for pleasure and enjoy together the whimsical illustrations. Then reread the story, emphasizing the initial G/g sound in the appropriate words. Ask children to listen closely for and identify all the words that start with G/g. Point out these words in the text, and make a list of them.

- Write each of the words from your list on an unlined index card. Read each word on the cards aloud with children. On another reading of the story, children can match the words on the index cards with the words in the story.

- Read aloud the cheer on page 120 several times, with lots of energy and enthusiasm. Invite children to join you in reciting the cheer when they feel ready. Encourage them to find any new G/g words in the cheer. Again, add these words to your list.

- Don't let your exploration of the letter G/g end with the story! Display your list of words in a place where children can easily see it. During the rest of the day or week, children can add new G/g words that they encounter in other books, on signs, on food labels, and so on.

On Monday, I went to the zoo.
Guess who followed me home?

A gorilla!
I asked my mom if he could stay.
"If he is a good guest," Mom said.

On Tuesday, Gorilla broke Granny's glasses and gabbed on the phone all day.

On Wednesday, Gorilla trampled
the grapes growing in the garden.

On Thursday, Gorilla gobbled up
a gooseberry pie, a gallon of ice cream,
and other goodies.

On Friday, Gorilla dressed like a ghost
and scared the goldfish.

On Saturday, Gorilla glued gumdrops to Dad's galoshes.

On Sunday, Gorilla invited a gang of
friends over. The gorillas played golf
and other games.

They made a great mess.

"That gorilla must go!" Mom said.

"He has been a terrible guest!"

On Monday, I went to visit Gorilla at the zoo.
Guess who followed me home?

Gg Cheer

G is for gorillas, on the loose.

G is for gopher, goldfish, and goose.

G is for granny, giggle, and glass.

G is for gumdrops, grapes, and grass.

Hooray for G, big and small—

the grandest, greatest letter of all!

Hide-and-Seek Hippo

By Samantha Berger

Illustrated by Maxie Chambliss

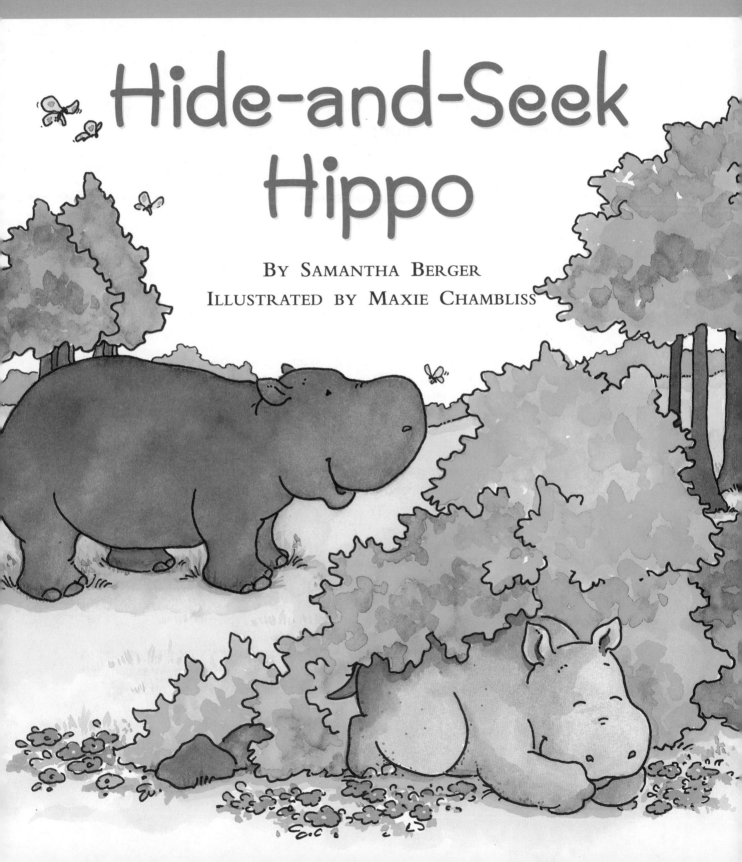

Reading Tips

Here are some quick and fun ways to use this story to help children build important alphabet recognition skills.

- Ask children to find big H and small h at the top of the previous page. Review the H/h sound with children. Can they find two words in the title that begin with the letter H/h? Read the title aloud, emphasizing the H/h sound as appropriate.

- Ask children to point out words they hear or see that begin with H/h. Explain that the story you are about to read includes many more words that begin with the letter H/h. Can they help you find them?

- Read the story aloud once for pleasure and enjoy together the whimsical illustrations. Then reread the story, emphasizing the initial H/h sound in the appropriate words. Ask children to listen closely for and identify all the words that start with H/h. Point out these words in the text, and make a list of them.

- Write each of the words from your list on an unlined index card. Read each word on the cards aloud with children. On another reading of the story, children can match the words on the index cards with the words in the story.

- Read aloud the cheer on page 136 several times, with lots of energy and enthusiasm. Invite children to join you in reciting the cheer when they feel ready. Encourage them to find any new H/h words in the cheer. Again, add these words to your list.

- Don't let your exploration of the letter H/h end with the story! Display your list of words in a place where children can easily see it. During the rest of the day or week, children can add new H/h words that they encounter in other books, on signs, on food labels, and so on.

Have you seen Baby Hippo?
It's time for him to come home.

He must be here somewhere!

Is he hiding in Hummingbird's honeysuckle?

Is he hiding in Hedgehog's hole?

Is he hiding in Hare's hutch?

Is he hiding in the hens' house?

Is he hiding in Horse's haystack?

Is he hiding behind the honeybees' hive?

Is he hiding in the hyenas' hideaway?

133

Where could Baby Hippo be hiding?
Mother Hippo has something for him...

...a great big hippo hug!

Hh Cheer

H is for honeybee, H is for hen.

H is for hamster and hogs in a pen.

H is for hiccups, hat, hug, and horse.

H is for hula-hoop and hippo, of course.

Hooray for H, big and small—

the happiest, hoppiest letter of all!

AlphaTales

Iguana on Ice

BY CAROL PUGLIANO-MARTIN
ILLUSTRATED BY ELLEN JOY SASAKI

Reading Tips

Here are some quick and fun ways to use this story to help children build important alphabet recognition skills.

- Ask children to find big I and small i at the top of the previous page. Review the long I/i and short I/i sounds with children. Can they find two words in the title that begin with the letter I/i? Read the title aloud, emphasizing the I/i sound as appropriate.

- Ask children to point out words they hear or see that begin with I/i. Explain that the story you are about to read includes many more words that begin with the letter I/i. Can they help you find them?

- Read the story aloud once for pleasure and enjoy together the whimsical illustrations. Then reread the story, emphasizing the initial I/i sound in the appropriate words. Ask children to listen closely for and identify all the words that start with I/i. Point out these words in the text, and make a list of them.

- Write each of the words from your list on an unlined index card. Read each word on the cards aloud with children. On another reading of the story, children can match the words on the index cards with the words in the story.

- Read aloud the cheer on page 152 several times, with lots of energy and enthusiasm. Invite children to join you in reciting the cheer when they feel ready. Encourage them to find any new I/i words in the cheer. Again, add these words to your list.

- Don't let your exploration of the letter I/i end with the story! Display your list of words in a place where children can easily see it. During the rest of the day or week, children can add new I/i words that they encounter in other books, on signs, on food labels, and so on.

Iggy Iguana lives on an island.

Iggy's island is very hot.
The heat makes Iggy feel ill.

To stay cool, Iggy floats in his inner tube.

Iggy imagines icy things.
He imagines eating ice cream.

Iggy imagines ice skating.

Iggy imagines floating on an iceberg.

Iggy imagines licking icicles.

Iggy even imagines sitting in front of an icebox with ice cubes!

One day, Iggy gets a postcard
from his cousin Izzy in Iceland.

The postcard gives Iggy an idea.
"I'll go to Iceland to visit Izzy!" says Iggy.

Now Iggy is in Iceland with Izzy.

Iggy eats ice cream.

Iggy ice skates.

Iggy floats on icebergs.

Iggy licks icicles.

And every night, Iggy sleeps
inside Iggy's igloo—
which is even better than an icebox!

Ii Cheer

I is for iguana and ice cream, too.

I is for island in the ocean blue.

I is for igloo and ivy patch.

I is for icicle and an itch to scratch.

Hooray for **I**, big and small—

the most incredible letter of all!

Jaguar's Jungleberry Jamboree

By Helen H. Moore
Illustrated by Ellen Joy Sasaki

Reading Tips

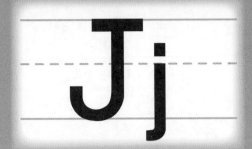

Here are some quick and fun ways to use this story to help children build important alphabet recognition skills.

- Ask children to find big J and small j at the top of the previous page. Review the J/j sound with children. Can they find three words in the title that begin with the letter J/j? Read the title aloud, emphasizing the J/j sound as appropriate.

- Ask children to point out words they hear or see that begin with J/j. Explain that the story you are about to read includes many more words that begin with the letter J/j. Can they help you find them?

- Read the story aloud once for pleasure and enjoy together the whimsical illustrations. Then reread the story, emphasizing the initial J/j sound in the appropriate words. Ask children to listen closely for and identify all the words that start with J/j. Point out these words in the text, and make a list of them.

- Write each of the words from your list on an unlined index card. Read each word on the cards aloud with children. On another reading of the story, children can match the words on the index cards with the words in the story.

- Read aloud the cheer on page 168 several times, with lots of energy and enthusiasm. Invite children to join you in reciting the cheer when they feel ready. Encourage them to find any new J/j words in the cheer. Again, add these words to your list.

- Don't let your exploration of the letter J/j end with the story! Display your list of words in a place where children can easily see it. During the rest of the day or week, children can add new J/j words that they encounter in other books, on signs, on food labels, and so on.

Jeremy Jaguar loved jam.
Jungleberry jam was Jeremy's favorite.

Jeremy loved jam on toast,

jam on pancakes,

jam on muffins,

even jam on ham!

One day, a terrible thing happened.
Jeremy Jaguar ran out of jam!

"I must pick some jungleberries
to make more jam," said Jeremy.
Jeremy waited until the first day of July,
when the jungleberries would be ripe.

Jeremy put on his jersey and jumped
in his jeep. He drove through the jungle
to the place where the jungleberry trees grew.

Soon he saw the trees up ahead.
The jungleberries were as bright as jewels!

As Jeremy got closer to the jungleberry trees, he heard jazzy music playing.

Jeremy peeked through the bushes.

"Jumping June bugs!" said Jeremy.
"It's a jaguar jamboree!"
Jaguars from every part of the jungle
had come to pick jungleberries.

The jaguars were jumping,
jitterbugging, and jiving.
And best of all,
they were making jam!

Jeremy joined the jamboree.
He jumped. He jitterbugged. He jived.
And he ate jungleberry jam until
he thought he would burst.

When the jamboree was over, Jeremy packed
his jeep with jam jars and drove home.
Now every July, he joins the other jaguars
for the jungleberry jamboree. And the jaguar
who eats the most jam is always Jeremy!

Jj Cheer

J is for jaguars, jumping high.

J is for jam, jeep, and July.

J is for jungle, jug, jar, and jeans.

J is for juice and jelly beans.

Hooray for **J**, big and small—

the jazziest, jolliest letter of all!

Kangaroo Kazoo

BY WENDY CHEYETTE LEWISON

ILLUSTRATED BY RUSTY FLETCHER

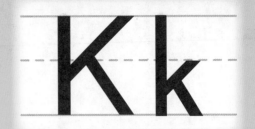

Reading Tips

Here are some quick and fun ways to use this story to help children build important alphabet recognition skills.

- Ask children to find big K and small k at the top of the previous page. Review the K/k sound with children. Can they find two words in the title that begin with the letter K/k? Read the title aloud, emphasizing the K/k sound as appropriate.

- Ask children to point out words they hear or see that begin with K/k. Explain that the story you are about to read includes many more words that begin with the letter K/k. Can they help you find them?

- Read the story aloud once for pleasure and enjoy together the whimsical illustrations. Then reread the story, emphasizing the initial K/k sound in the appropriate words. Ask children to listen closely for and identify all the words that start with K/k. Point out these words in the text, and make a list of them.

- Write each of the words from your list on an unlined index card. Read each word on the cards aloud with children. On another reading of the story, children can match the words on the index cards with the words in the story.

- Read aloud the cheer on page 184 several times, with lots of energy and enthusiasm. Invite children to join you in reciting the cheer when they feel ready. Encourage them to find any new K/k words in the cheer. Again, add these words to your list.

- Don't let your exploration of the letter K/k end with the story! Display your list of words in a place where children can easily see it. During the rest of the day or week, children can add new K/k words that they encounter in other books, on signs, on food labels, and so on.

This kangaroo has a red kazoo.
She takes it everywhere.

This kangaroo has a pink kazoo.
He plays it at the fair.

This kangaroo has a yellow kazoo.
She plays it in the spring.

This kangaroo has a green kazoo.
It makes the katydids sing.

This kangaroo has a blue kazoo
to play on the deep blue sea.

This kangaroo has a purple kazoo
from the purple kazooka tree.

This kangaroo has an orange kazoo,
and now he has a chance...

...to join the best band in the land

and play at the kangaroo dance.

They play all day,
they never stop,
while the kangaroo king
does the kangaroo hop.

Then the king's kooky kin
all kick up their heels.
They do the kazooky-pooky
and the kazarama reel.

Red or yellow, green or orange,
purple, pink, or blue—

you can have all kinds of fun
with a kangaroo kazoo!

Kk Cheer

K is for king and kangaroo.
K is for kettle, key, and kazoo.
K is for koala, K is for kite.
K is for a kiss goodnight.
Hooray for K, big and small—
the kookiest, kickiest letter of all!

The Lamb Who Loved to Laugh

By Carol Pugliano-Martin

Illustrated by Hans Wilhelm

Here are some quick and fun ways to use this story to help children build important alphabet recognition skills.

- Ask children to find big L and small l at the top of the previous page. Review the L/l sound with children. Can they find three words in the title that begin with the letter L/l? Read the title aloud, emphasizing the L/l sound as appropriate.

- Ask children to point out words they hear or see that begin with L/l. Explain that the story you are about to read includes many more words that begin with the letter L/l. Can they help you find them?

- Read the story aloud once for pleasure and enjoy together the whimsical illustrations. Then reread the story, emphasizing the initial L/l sound in the appropriate words. Ask children to listen closely for and identify all the words that start with L/l. Point out these words in the text, and make a list of them.

- Write each of the words from your list on an unlined index card. Read each word on the cards aloud with children. On another reading of the story, children can match the words on the index cards with the words in the story.

- Read aloud the cheer on page 200 several times, with lots of energy and enthusiasm. Invite children to join you in reciting the cheer when they feel ready. Encourage them to find any new L/l words in the cheer. Again, add these words to your list.

- Don't let your exploration of the letter L/l end with the story! Display your list of words in a place where children can easily see it. During the rest of the day or week, children can add new L/l words that they encounter in other books, on signs, on food labels, and so on.

Lulu the Lamb loved to laugh.

Lulu laughed at Ladybug
because she was so little.

Lulu laughed at Llama when he spilled pink lemonade at lunch.

Lulu laughed at Lizard
when she fell off the ladder.

Lulu laughed at Leopard's
lavender leotard.

The other animals did not like Lulu's laughing.
It made them feel low.
"Someday, Lulu will learn," said Leopard.

Lulu walked along, laughing loudly.
She bumped into Lion,
who was licking a lollipop.
The lollipop got stuck in Lion's mane!

Lulu laughed at Lion.
She laughed and laughed and laughed.

Lion looked angry. He roared at Lulu.
Lion roared so loud, he made Lulu fall...
right into the lake!

Ladybug, Llama, Lizard, Leopard,
and Lion laughed at Lulu.
Lulu didn't like being laughed
at one little bit!

"From now on, I will laugh less,"
Lulu promised her friends.
"At last, Lulu has learned her lesson!"
said Ladybug.

Lulu still likes to laugh at her friends...

but only when they tell her a funny joke!

Ll Cheer

L is for lamb and licorice stick.

L is for lots of lollipops to lick.

L is for lion and ladybug.

L is for leaf and lemonade in a jug.

Hooray for L, big and small—

the loveliest, luckiest letter of all!

Monkey's Miserable Monday

By Valerie Garfield
Illustrated by James Young

Reading Tips

Here are some quick and fun ways to use this story to help children build important alphabet recognition skills.

- Ask children to find big M and small m at the top of the previous page. Review the M/m sound with children. Can they find three words in the title that begin with the letter M/m? Read the title aloud, emphasizing the M/m sound as appropriate.

- Ask children to point out words they hear or see that begin with M/m. Explain that the story you are about to read includes many more words that begin with the letter M/m. Can they help you find them?

- Read the story aloud once for pleasure and enjoy together the whimsical illustrations. Then reread the story, emphasizing the initial M/m sound in the appropriate words. Ask children to listen closely for and identify all the words that start with M/m. Point out these words in the text, and make a list of them.

- Write each of the words from your list on an unlined index card. Read each word on the cards aloud with children. On another reading of the story, children can match the words on the index cards with the words in the story.

- Read aloud the cheer on page 216 several times, with lots of energy and enthusiasm. Invite children to join you in reciting the cheer when they feel ready. Encourage them to find any new M/m words in the cheer. Again, add these words to your list.

- Don't let your exploration of the letter M/m end with the story! Display your list of words in a place where children can easily see it. During the rest of the day or week, children can add new M/m words that they encounter in other books, on signs, on food labels, and so on.

Monkey is in a bad mood.
He woke up late and now he must hurry
or he'll miss the school bus.
"This Monday morning is off to
a miserable start!" Monkey mutters.

The bus will be here in a few minutes, but Monkey can't find any socks that match. "What a miserable Monday!" Monkey mutters.

At breakfast, Monkey spills the milk.
"What a miserable Monday!"
Monkey mutters as he mops up the mess.

Monkey has misplaced his lunch money,
so he must make a sandwich.
But there is no lunch meat, only mustard.
"What a miserable Monday!"
Monkey mutters.

It is snowing outside.
Monkey can't find his mittens anywhere.
"What a miserable Monday!"
Monkey mutters.

Monkey looks over his math homework.
He sees two mistakes!
"What a miserable Monday!"
Monkey mutters.

Monkey runs out the door
to catch the bus. Whoops!
He trips on the mat.

All of his marbles roll out of his bag.
Monkey is mad.
"I hate Mondays!" Monkey moans.

Monkey's mother comes to the door.
"What's the matter, my little monkey?"
she asks.

Monkey tells his mother about the
socks that don't match, the spilled milk,
the mustard sandwich, the mistakes
on his math homework, the lost mittens,
the mat, and the marbles.

"Now I'm going to miss the bus!"
Monkey moans. "What a miserable Monday!"
Monkey's mother gives him a hug and smiles.
"But munchkin, today isn't Monday," she says.
"It's only Sunday!"

Monkey's mother makes him
a mug of cocoa with mini marshmallows.
Then she mixes up a batch of
maple muffins—Monkey's favorite!

Monkey spends the rest of the morning
drawing meadows and mountains with
his magic markers. "What a MARVELOUS
Sunday," says Monkey. And it is.

Mm Cheer

M is for monkey, marbles, and mop.

M is for mitten and mountaintop.

M is for mouse and the moon in the sky.

M is for muffin, milk, and mud pie.

Hooray for M, big and small—

the most magical, marvelous letter of all!

The Nicest Newt

By Heather Feldman

Illustrated by Paul Harvey

Here are some quick and fun ways to use this story to help children build important alphabet recognition skills.

- Ask children to find big N and small n at the top of the previous page. Review the N/n sound with children. Can they find two words in the title that begin with the letter N/n? Read the title aloud, emphasizing the N/n sound as appropriate.

- Ask children to point out words they hear or see that begin with N/n. Explain that the story you are about to read includes many more words that begin with the letter N/n. Can they help you find them?

- Read the story aloud once for pleasure and enjoy together the whimsical illustrations. Then reread the story, emphasizing the initial N/n sound in the appropriate words. Ask children to listen closely for and identify all the words that start with N/n. Point out these words in the text, and make a list of them.

- Write each of the words from your list on an unlined index card. Read each word on the cards aloud with children. On another reading of the story, children can match the words on the index cards with the words in the story.

- Read aloud the cheer on page 232 several times, with lots of energy and enthusiasm. Invite children to join you in reciting the cheer when they feel ready. Encourage them to find any new N/n words in the cheer. Again, add these words to your list.

- Don't let your exploration of the letter N/n end with the story! Display your list of words in a place where children can easily see it. During the rest of the day or week, children can add new N/n words that they encounter in other books, on signs, on food labels, and so on.

Nate is a very nice newt.

Nate brings his father the newspaper.

Nate helps his neighbors.

Nate is never noisy when his mother
is working.

At noon, Nate neatly folds the napkins
for lunch.

After lunch, Nate tucks his nine brothers in for a nap.

Nate helps his sister learn her numbers.

Nate always keeps his room neat.

Nate loans his friend Natalie a nickel
so she can buy a new necklace.

Being nice can make a newt hungry.
Nate needs a snack.
He sees a cake that Nana Newt
has made for dessert.

Nate nibbles and nibbles on the cake.
Soon, there is none left.

Sometimes, even nice newts are naughty.

Nn Cheer

N is for newt, noodle, and nose.

N is for needle to sew torn clothes.

N is for newspaper, nut, nail, and nest.

N is for nap, when you need to rest.

Hooray for N, big and small—

the niftiest, neatest letter of all!

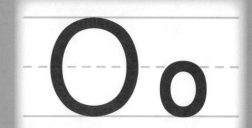

Olive the Octopus's Day of Juggling

BY LIZA CHARLESWORTH
ILLUSTRATED BY MATT PHILLIPS

Reading Tips

Here are some quick and fun ways to use this story to help children build important alphabet recognition skills.

- Ask children to find big O and small o at the top of the previous page. Review the long O/o and short O/o sounds with children. Can they find three words in the title that begin with the letter O/o? Read the title aloud, emphasizing the O/o sound as appropriate.

- Ask children to point out words they hear or see that begin with O/o. Explain that the story you are about to read includes many more words that begin with the letter O/o. Can they help you find them?

- Read the story aloud once for pleasure and enjoy together the whimsical illustrations. Then reread the story, emphasizing the initial O/o sound in the appropriate words. Ask children to listen closely for and identify all the words that start with O/o. Point out these words in the text, and make a list of them.

- Write each of the words from your list on an unlined index card. Read each word on the cards aloud with children. On another reading of the story, children can match the words on the index cards with the words in the story.

- Read aloud the cheer on page 248 several times, with lots of energy and enthusiasm. Invite children to join you in reciting the cheer when they feel ready. Encourage them to find any new O/o words in the cheer. Again, add these words to your list.

- Don't let your exploration of the letter O/o end with the story! Display your list of words in a place where children can easily see it. During the rest of the day or week, children can add new O/o words that they encounter in other books, on signs, on food labels, and so on.

Olive is an octopus.
She lives in the ocean.

Olive dreams of becoming a juggler.
She practices around the clock.

At one o'clock, Olive juggles an onion.

At two o'clock, Olive juggles an onion
and an old pair of overalls.

At three o'clock, Olive adds an owl
in an oak tree.

At four o'clock, Olive adds an orangutan.

At five o'clock, Olive adds an orange alien
from outer space.

At six o'clock, Olive adds
an entire orchestra.

At seven o'clock, Olive gets
oh so sleepy and...OOOPS!
Down come the onion
and the old pair of overalls

and the owl in the oak tree and the orangutan and the orange alien from outer space and even the entire orchestra— right on Olive's head!

Now, Olive dreams of becoming an organist.
She practices around the clock.

Oo Cheer

O is for octopus who lives in the sea.

O is for owl, high in a tree.

O is for overalls and oars for a boat.

O is for ostrich, orange, and oat.

Hooray for O, big and small—

the most outstanding letter of all!

AlphaTales

The Pigs' Picnic

By Helen H. Moore

Illustrated by Ellen Joy Sasaki

Reading Tips

Here are some quick and fun ways to use this story to help children build important alphabet recognition skills.

- Ask children to find big P and small p at the top of the previous page. Review the P/p sound with children. Can they find two words in the title that begin with the letter P/p? Read the title aloud, emphasizing the P/p sound as appropriate.

- Ask children to point out words they hear or see that begin with P/p. Explain that the story you are about to read includes many more words that begin with the letter P/p. Can they help you find them?

- Read the story aloud once for pleasure and enjoy together the whimsical illustrations. Then reread the story, emphasizing the initial P/p sound in the appropriate words. Ask children to listen closely for and identify all the words that start with P/p. Point out these words in the text, and make a list of them.

- Write each of the words from your list on an unlined index card. Read each word on the cards aloud with children. On another reading of the story, children can match the words on the index cards with the words in the story.

- Read aloud the cheer on page 264 several times, with lots of energy and enthusiasm. Invite children to join you in reciting the cheer when they feel ready. Encourage them to find any new P/p words in the cheer. Again, add these words to your list.

- Don't let your exploration of the letter P/p end with the story! Display your list of words in a place where children can easily see it. During the rest of the day or week, children can add new P/p words that they encounter in other books, on signs, on food labels, and so on.

Penny, Polly, and Peter Pig were
planning a picnic.
"What shall we pack in our picnic basket?"
asked Penny.

Peter looked in the pantry.

"Let's pack some peaches," said Peter.

"A peachy idea!" said Polly.

"Are they ripe?" asked Penny.

"Perhaps we should taste them first,"
said Polly.

And they did.
"Perfect!" said Penny.

"Let's pack pickles," said Peter.
"Perhaps we should taste the pickles, too,"
said Polly.

And they did.

"MMMMMMM. Pickle-icious!" said Peter.

Peter made some peanut butter
and potato chip sandwiches.
"Would you like to taste them?"
Peter asked Penny and Polly.

"Yes, please!" said Penny and Polly.
And they did.

"Perhaps we should pack
some pasta salad," said Polly.
"And pears and plums," said Penny.

"And pumpkin pie," said Peter.
Of course, Penny, Polly, and Peter
tasted everything first.

Before long, the pantry was empty.
But so was the picnic basket!
Penny, Polly, and Peter were puzzled.

"That's peculiar!" said Peter.
"I guess we'll have to put off
our picnic," said Polly.
"We could order pizza instead," said Penny.

And they did!

Pp Cheer

P is for pig, pickles, and pot.

P is for pizza, gooey and hot.

P is for pancakes, piled up high.

P is for puppy, popcorn, and pie.

Hooray for **P**, big and small—

the peachiest, peppiest letter of all!

The Quiet Quail

BY HEATHER FELDMAN

ILLUSTRATED BY RUSTY FLETCHER

Reading Tips

Here are some quick and fun ways to use this story to help children build important alphabet recognition skills.

- Ask children to find big Q and small q at the top of the previous page. Review the Q/q sound with children. Can they find two words in the title that begin with the letter Q/q? Read the title aloud, emphasizing the Q/q sound as appropriate.

- Ask children to point out words they hear or see that begin with Q/q. Explain that the story you are about to read includes many more words that begin with the letter Q/q. Can they help you find them?

- Read the story aloud once for pleasure and enjoy together the whimsical illustrations. Then reread the story, emphasizing the initial Q/q sound in the appropriate words. Ask children to listen closely for and identify all the words that start with Q/q. Point out these words in the text, and make a list of them.

- Write each of the words from your list on an unlined index card. Read each word on the cards aloud with children. On another reading of the story, children can match the words on the index cards with the words in the story.

- Read aloud the cheer on page 280 several times, with lots of energy and enthusiasm. Invite children to join you in reciting the cheer when they feel ready. Encourage them to find any new Q/q words in the cheer. Again, add these words to your list.

- Don't let your exploration of the letter Q/q end with the story! Display your list of words in a place where children can easily see it. During the rest of the day or week, children can add new Q/q words that they encounter in other books, on signs, on food labels, and so on.

Quincy is a quiet quail.
He likes to do quiet things.
Quincy likes to snuggle with his favorite quilt
and listen to the quiet pitter-pat of the rain.

Quincy likes to sit quietly and read.

Quincy likes to take quiet walks.

Sometimes on his quiet walks,
Quincy meets his friend Dottie Duck.
Dottie is not very quiet.
In fact, Dottie is quite loud.

"QUACK! QUACK! QUACK! HI, QUINCY!
QUACK, QUACK!" shouts Dottie.
"Hello, Dottie," whispers the quiet quail.

Quincy and Dottie sit in the park.
"QUACK! QUACK! QUACK! QUACK! QUACK!"
shouts Dottie. "WHAT A BEAUTIFUL DAY!
QUACK! QUACK!"

Dottie quacks and quacks
till Quincy's head hurts.
"Dottie, please quit quacking," says Quincy.
But Dottie is quacking so loudly, she does not
hear the quiet quail.

Quincy decides to go for a swim to drown out Dottie's quacking. He spreads his quilt on the grass and jumps in the pond.

Suddenly, Queenie the dog trots by.
She grabs Quincy's quilt and runs away.
"My quilt!" cries Quincy. "Someone stop
Queenie!" But Quincy's voice is too quiet.
No one hears him.

Queenie runs right past Dottie.
"THAT'S QUINCY'S QUILT!" quacks Dottie.
"CATCH QUEENIE! QUICK!"

The other animals hear Dottie's loud quacking. They chase Queenie.

Queenie is quick, but the other animals are quicker. They snatch Quincy's quilt from Queenie's teeth. They give the quilt back to Quincy.

Quincy thanks all the animals for rescuing her quilt, especially Dottie. "Your loud quacking saved the day!" Quincy tells Dottie. And for once, the quiet quail is happy to have such a noisy friend.

Qq Cheer

Q is for quail and a quilt for your bed.
Q is for queen, with a crown on her head.
Q is for quack and a quarter to spend.
Q is for a quarrel you have with a friend.
Hooray for Q, big and small—
the quaintest, quirkiest letter of all!

AlphaTales

Rr

Rosie Rabbit's Radish

By Wendy Cheyette Lewison

Illustrated by Rusty Fletcher

Reading Tips

Here are some quick and fun ways to use this story to help children build important alphabet recognition skills.

- Ask children to find big R and small r at the top of the previous page. Review the R/r sound with children. Can they find three words in the title that begin with the letter R/r? Read the title aloud, emphasizing the R/r sound as appropriate.

- Ask children to point out words they hear or see that begin with R/r. Explain that the story you are about to read includes many more words that begin with the letter R/r. Can they help you find them?

- Read the story aloud once for pleasure and enjoy together the whimsical illustrations. Then reread the story, emphasizing the initial R/r sound in the appropriate words. Ask children to listen closely for and identify all the words that start with R/r. Point out these words in the text, and make a list of them.

- Write each of the words from your list on an unlined index card. Read each word on the cards aloud with children. On another reading of the story, children can match the words on the index cards with the words in the story.

- Read aloud the cheer on page 296 several times, with lots of energy and enthusiasm. Invite children to join you in reciting the cheer when they feel ready. Encourage them to find any new R/r words in the cheer. Again, add these words to your list.

- Don't let your exploration of the letter R/r end with the story! Display your list of words in a place where children can easily see it. During the rest of the day or week, children can add new R/r words that they encounter in other books, on signs, on food labels, and so on.

Rosie Rabbit has a radish.

Rosie takes good care of her radish.
She rakes the ground around it.
She removes rocks.

Rosie rakes and rakes—even in the rain!
She does not rest.

"Come for a ride," says Rick Rooster.
"Let's roller-skate," says Rita Raccoon.

But Rosie would rather take care
of her radish.

At night, Rosie sits in her rocking chair.
She reads to her radish and plays the radio.

The radish grows and grows.
Soon the radish is ripe.
It is ready to be picked.

Rosie ties a rope around the radish.
Rick and Rita help her pull up the radish root.

What a rare radish!
It is red and round and really big!

Rick and Rita help Rosie roll the radish
down the road.

What will Rosie do with her radish?

She will take it to the fair...

and win a blue ribbon!

Rr Cheer

R is for rabbit, radish, and rose.

R is for ribbon and the rooster that crows.

R is for run, rope, rock, and red.

R is for raindrops that fall on your head.

Hooray for **R**, big and small—

the most remarkable letter of all!

S s

Seal's Silly Sandwich

By Dorothy J. Sklar

Illustrated by Paul Harvey

Reading Tips

Here are some quick and fun ways to use this story to help children build important alphabet recognition skills.

- Ask children to find big S and small s at the top of the previous page. Review the S/s sound with children. Can they find three words in the title that begin with the letter S/s? Read the title aloud, emphasizing the S/s sound as appropriate.

- Ask children to point out words they hear or see that begin with S/s. Explain that the story you are about to read includes many more words that begin with the letter S/s. Can they help you find them?

- Read the story aloud once for pleasure and enjoy together the whimsical illustrations. Then reread the story, emphasizing the initial S/s sound in the appropriate words. Ask children to listen closely for and identify all the words that start with S/s. Point out these words in the text, and make a list of them.

- Write each of the words from your list on an unlined index card. Read each word on the cards aloud with children. On another reading of the story, children can match the words on the index cards with the words in the story.

- Read aloud the cheer on page 312 several times, with lots of energy and enthusiasm. Invite children to join you in reciting the cheer when they feel ready. Encourage them to find any new S/s words in the cheer. Again, add these words to your list.

- Don't let your exploration of the letter S/s end with the story! Display your list of words in a place where children can easily see it. During the rest of the day or week, children can add new S/s words that they encounter in other books, on signs, on food labels, and so on.

One Sunday, Seal invited his friends
for supper.

"What's for supper?" said Snail.
"I am serving a sandwich," said Seal.

Seal put some sardines on a slice of bread.
"Sardines in a sandwich!" said Snail.
"That's silly!"

Next Seal added some stew.
"Stew in a sandwich!" said Sloth.
"That's silly!"

Next Seal added some spaghetti.
"Spaghetti in a sandwich!" said Snake.
"That's silly!"

Next Seal added some spinach.
"Spinach in a sandwich!" said Salamander.
"That's silly!"

Next Seal added some scrambled eggs.
"Scrambled eggs in a sandwich!" said Skunk.
"That's silly!"

Next Seal added six scoops
of strawberry ice cream.
"Strawberry ice cream in a sandwich!"
said Spider. "That's silly!"

Next Seal added some salsa
and some maple syrup.
"Salsa and syrup in a sandwich!"
said Squirrel. "That's silly!"

"Who's ready for a slice of my sandwich?"
said Seal.

"No thanks," said Snail, Sloth, Snake, Salamander, Skunk, Spider, and Squirrel. "That sandwich is just too silly!"

But Seal didn't think his sandwich
was silly at all.

He thought it was scrumptious!

Ss Cheer

S is for spider, snake, snail, and seal.

S is for a super-sized sandwich meal.

S is for sailboat, smile, and sing.

S is for spaghetti, seesaw, and swing.

Hooray for S, big and small—

the most sensational letter of all!

AlphaTales

T t

When Tilly Turtle Came to Tea

By Carol Pugliano-Martin

Illustrated by Rusty Fletcher

Reading Tips

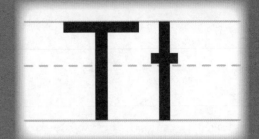

Here are some quick and fun ways to use this story to help children build important alphabet recognition skills.

- Ask children to find big T and small t at the top of the previous page. Review the T/t sound with children. Can they find four words in the title that begin with the letter T/t? Read the title aloud, emphasizing the T/t sound as appropriate.

- Ask children to point out words they hear or see that begin with T/t. Explain that the story you are about to read includes many more words that begin with the letter T/t. Can they help you find them?

- Read the story aloud once for pleasure and enjoy together the whimsical illustrations. Then reread the story, emphasizing the initial T/t sound in the appropriate words. Ask children to listen closely for and identify all the words that start with T/t. Point out these words in the text, and make a list of them.

- Write each of the words from your list on an unlined index card. Read each word on the cards aloud with children. On another reading of the story, children can match the words on the index cards with the words in the story.

- Read aloud the cheer on page 328 several times, with lots of energy and enthusiasm. Invite children to join you in reciting the cheer when they feel ready. Encourage them to find any new T/t words in the cheer. Again, add these words to your list.

- Don't let your exploration of the letter T/t end with the story! Display your list of words in a place where children can easily see it. During the rest of the day or week, children can add new T/t words that they encounter in other books, on signs, on food labels, and so on.

When Tilly Turtle came to tea,
She took a taxi to the tree,
Where the party was to be,
When Tilly Turtle came to tea.

When Tilly Turtle came to tea,
She arrived on time at three,

Looking pretty as could be,
When Tilly Turtle came to tea.

When Tilly Turtle came to tea,
There were tiny teacups set for three,

And toast and tarts beneath the tree,
When Tilly Turtle came to tea.

When Tilly Turtle came to tea,
Her friends Tiger and Toad and she,
Told tall tales and laughed with glee,
When Tilly Turtle came to tea.

When Tilly Turtle came to tea,
She laughed so hard she could not see,
And tipped the table with her knee,
When Tilly Turtle came to tea.

When Tilly Turtle came to tea,
The teacups tumbled, oh dear me!

What a terrible sight to see!
When Tilly Turtle came to tea.

When Tilly Turtle came to tea,
She told her friends, "Please pardon me,
For the topsy-turvy mess you see!"
When Tilly Turtle came to tea.

When Tilly Turtle came to tea,
She said, "If you will both agree,
Please put the tablecloth on me!"
When Tilly Turtle came to tea.

When Tilly Turtle came to tea,
She saved the party cheerfully.

She turned into a table—see?
When Tilly Turtle came to tea.

Tt Cheer

T is for turtle, tiger, and toad.
T is for taxi driving down the road.
T is for table and telephone booth.
T is for teacup, tickle, and tooth.
Hooray for T, big and small—
the most totally terrific letter of all!

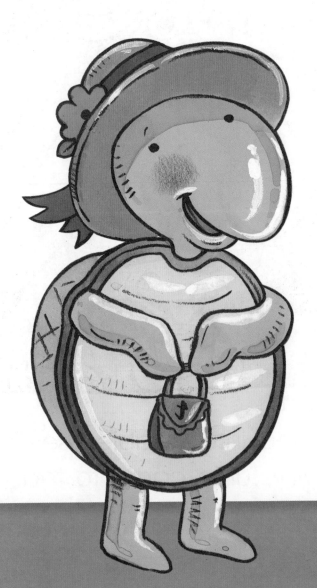

Umbrellabird's Umbrella

BY HEATHER FELDMAN

ILLUSTRATED BY NADINE BERNARD WESTCOTT

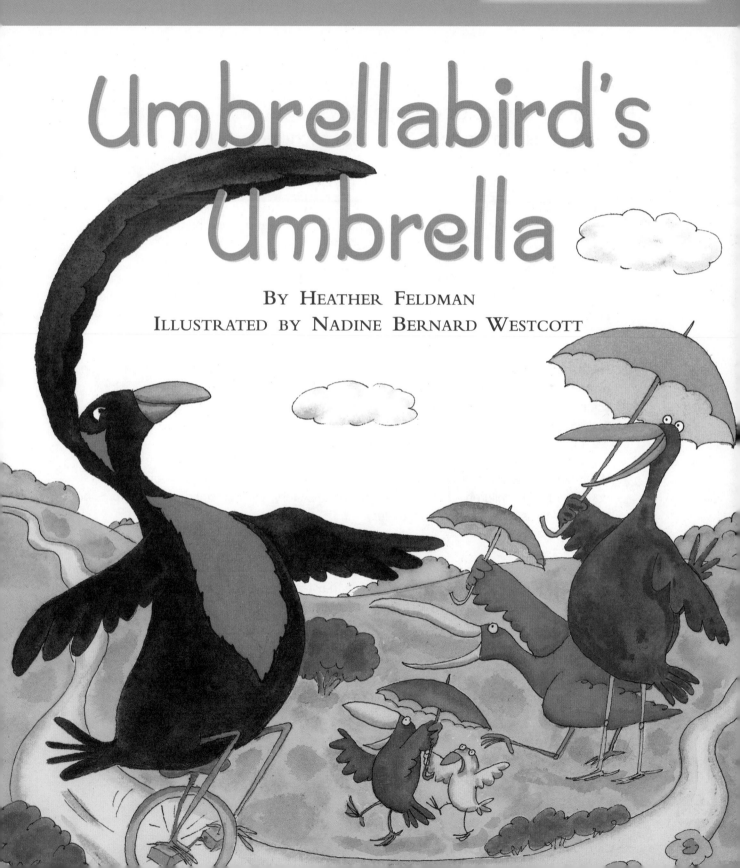

Here are some quick and fun ways to use this story to help children build important alphabet recognition skills.

- Ask children to find big U and small u at the top of the previous page. Review the long U/u and short U/u sounds with children. Can they find two words in the title that begin with the letter U/u? Read the title aloud, emphasizing the U/u sound as appropriate.

- Ask children to point out words they hear or see that begin with U/u. Explain that the story you are about to read includes many more words that begin with the letter U/u. Can they help you find them?

- Read the story aloud once for pleasure and enjoy together the whimsical illustrations. Then reread the story, emphasizing the initial U/u sound in the appropriate words. Ask children to listen closely for and identify all the words that start with U/u. Point out these words in the text, and make a list of them.

- Write each of the words from your list on an unlined index card. Read each word on the cards aloud with children. On another reading of the story, children can match the words on the index cards with the words in the story.

- Read aloud the cheer on page 344 several times, with lots of energy and enthusiasm. Invite children to join you in reciting the cheer when they feel ready. Encourage them to find any new U/u words in the cheer. Again, add these words to your list.

- Don't let your exploration of the letter U/u end with the story! Display your list of words in a place where children can easily see it. During the rest of the day or week, children can add new U/u words that they encounter in other books, on signs, on food labels, and so on.

Umbrellabird is unlike any other bird.
He has very unusual feathers.

The other birds tease Umbrellabird about his unusual feathers. They think his feathers look like a giant umbrella.

"Why is your umbrella up?"
the other birds ask Umbrellabird.
"Is it going to rain today?"

The teasing makes Umbrellabird very unhappy.
He tries to hide his feathers under a hat.
But it is no use. His umbrella always pops up.

One day, Umbrellabird decides to visit his uncle.
He hops on his unicycle and pedals uptown.

"Look at those ugly feathers!"
the other birds call as Umbrellabird rides by.
Umbrellabird pretends not to hear them.

He looks up at the sky
and keeps on pedaling.
"Uh-oh!" says Umbrellabird.
He sees dark clouds, way up high.

Suddenly, it begins to pour.
But Umbrellabird notices that he
is not getting wet. Umbrellabird's umbrella
is keeping him dry!

The other birds look for a dry place.
Umbrellabird calls to them.
"Come under my umbrella.
It's dry under here!"

"Quickly! Quickly!" says Umbrellabird
as the other birds duck under his feathers.
The birds stay under Umbrellabird's umbrella
until the rain stops.

All the birds thank Umbrellabird.

"Your wonderful umbrella kept us dry," they say.

"We are sorry we upset you with our teasing.

We wish we had umbrellas like you!"

Now Umbrellabird holds his head up high when he is out riding his unicycle.

And sometimes, Umbrellabird even wishes
for a little rain!

Uu Cheer

U is for umbrellabird
and an umbrella to share.
U is for unicycle and underwear.
U is for unicorn, umpire, and us.
U is for uncle and uptown bus.
Hooray for U, big and small—
the most unbelievable letter of all!

Vera Viper's Valentine

BY MAXWELL HIGGINS

ILLUSTRATED BY JAMES YOUNG

Here are some quick and fun ways to use this story to help children build important alphabet recognition skills.

- Ask children to find big V and small v at the top of the previous page. Review the V/v sound with children. Can they find three words in the title that begin with the letter V/v? Read the title aloud, emphasizing the V/v sound as appropriate.

- Ask children to point out words they hear or see that begin with V/v. Explain that the story you are about to read includes many more words that begin with the letter V/v. Can they help you find them?

- Read the story aloud once for pleasure and enjoy together the whimsical illustrations. Then reread the story, emphasizing the initial V/v sound in the appropriate words. Ask children to listen closely for and identify all the words that start with V/v. Point out these words in the text, and make a list of them.

- Write each of the words from your list on an unlined index card. Read each word on the cards aloud with children. On another reading of the story, children can match the words on the index cards with the words in the story.

- Read aloud the cheer on page 360 several times, with lots of energy and enthusiasm. Invite children to join you in reciting the cheer when they feel ready. Encourage them to find any new V/v words in the cheer. Again, add these words to your list.

- Don't let your exploration of the letter V/v end with the story! Display your list of words in a place where children can easily see it. During the rest of the day or week, children can add new V/v words that they encounter in other books, on signs, on food labels, and so on.

Vera Viper and Victor Viper were best friends.
Every Sunday, Vera would visit Victor.

Vera and Victor would play volleyball...

...and watch videos.

Sometimes they would go for a drive
through the valley.

Vera and Victor liked to stop in the village
for vanilla ice cream cones.

One Sunday, Vera Viper knocked on Victor's door. "Vera, I cannot visit with you today," said Victor. "I am very, very busy."

The next Sunday, Victor was still busy.
And the Sunday after that, too.
Vera Viper was very, very sad.
"I don't think Victor wants
to be friends anymore," Vera said.

The next Sunday, Vera stayed home.
She watched videos, but it wasn't
any fun without Victor.
Then there was a knock at Vera's door.

It was Victor! Victor handed Vera
a big red valentine. "I'm sorry I haven't
been able to visit," said Victor. "I have
been busy making you this valentine."

Roses are red,

violets are blue,

I'm very glad I have

a best friend like you!

Victor read Vera the verse on the valentine.
"Thank you, Victor," said Vera.
"I am very glad you are my best friend, too!"

Then Vera and Victor played volleyball.

They watched videos.

They drove through the valley.

On the way home, Vera and Victor
stopped in the village
for vanilla ice creams cones.

And that Sunday, Vera was the
happiest viper in the whole world!

Vv Cheer

V is for viper and valentine, too.
V is for delicious vegetable stew.
V is for violin, village, and vase.
V is for van and vacation days.
Hooray for **V**, big and small—
the very, VERY best letter of all!

AlphaTales

Worm's Wagon

By Samantha Berger

Illustrated by Matt Phillips

Reading Tips

Here are some quick and fun ways to use this story to help children build important alphabet recognition skills.

- Ask children to find big W and small w at the top of the previous page. Review the W/w sound with children. Can they find two words in the title that begin with the letter W/w? Read the title aloud, emphasizing the W/w sound as appropriate.

- Ask children to point out words they hear or see that begin with W/w. Explain that the story you are about to read includes many more words that begin with the letter W/w. Can they help you find them?

- Read the story aloud once for pleasure and enjoy together the whimsical illustrations. Then reread the story, emphasizing the initial W/w sound in the appropriate words. Ask children to listen closely for and identify all the words that start with W/w. Point out these words in the text, and make a list of them.

- Write each of the words from your list on an unlined index card. Read each word on the cards aloud with children. On another reading of the story, children can match the words on the index cards with the words in the story.

- Read aloud the cheer on page 376 several times, with lots of energy and enthusiasm. Invite children to join you in reciting the cheer when they feel ready. Encourage them to find any new W/w words in the cheer. Again, add these words to your list.

- Don't let your exploration of the letter W/w end with the story! Display your list of words in a place where children can easily see it. During the rest of the day or week, children can add new W/w words that they encounter in other books, on signs, on food labels, and so on.

One day, Worm went to the woods
to gather walnuts.
He brought his wagon with him.

On his way home, Worm saw Woodpecker whistling in a weeping willow. Woodpecker asked Worm for a ride.

Worm wiggled along, pulling Woodpecker
in his wagon. Soon they came upon Weasel
eating watermelon.
Weasel asked Worm for a ride.

Worm wiggled along, pulling Woodpecker and Weasel in his wagon. Before long, they bumped into Wombat wearing her new wig. Wombat asked Worm for a ride.

Worm wiggled along, pulling Woodpecker, Weasel, and Wombat in his wagon. Next, they met Wolf on his way to work. Wolf asked Worm for a ride.

Worm wiggled along, pulling Woodpecker, Weasel, Wombat, and Wolf in his wagon. Soon they saw Walrus winking and waving. Walrus asked Worm for a ride.

Worm wiggled along, pulling Woodpecker, Weasel, Wombat, Wolf, and Walrus in his wagon. Up ahead, they saw Whale playing in the water. Whale asked Worm for a ride.

Worm wiggled with all his might trying
to pull Woodpecker, Weasel, Wombat,
Wolf, Walrus, and Whale in the wagon.
But the wagon would not move.
The wheels started to wobble.

WHAM!

The weight was too much for the wagon.

It crashed to the ground.

"Oh, no! My wagon!" Worm wailed.

"Don't worry, Worm," the animals said.

Worm's friends worked on the wagon
all afternoon.

When the wagon was fixed,
Worm wiggled into it.

Then Wombat, Weasel, Wolf, Woodpecker,
Walrus, and Whale pulled Worm
all the way home.
And weary Worm had a wonderful ride.

Ww Cheer

W is for worm and a wagon to pull.

W is for wig, whale, wave, and wool.

W is for watermelon, juicy and sweet.

W is for walnuts, waffles, and wheat.

Hooray for **W**, big and small—

the wildest, wackiest letter of all!

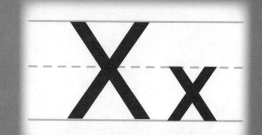

A Xylophone for X-Ray Fish

By Liza Charlesworth
Illustrated by James Young

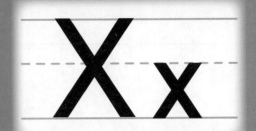

Here are some quick and fun ways to use this story to help children build important alphabet recognition skills.

- Ask children to find big X and small x at the top of the previous page. Review the sounds X/x makes (both /eks/ and /z/) with children. Can they find two words in the title that begin with the letter X/x? Read the title aloud, emphasizing the X/x sound as appropriate.

- Ask children to point out words they hear or see that begin with X/x and Ex/ex. Explain that the story you are about to read includes many more words that begin with the letter X/x and with Ex/ex. Can they help you find them?

- Read the story aloud once for pleasure and enjoy together the whimsical illustrations. Then reread the story, emphasizing the initial X/x sound in the appropriate words. Ask children to listen closely for and identify all the words that start with X/x and Ex/ex. Point out these words in the text, and make a list of them.

- Write each of the words from your list on an unlined index card. Read each word on the cards aloud with children. On another reading of the story, children can match the words on the index cards with the words in the story.

- Read aloud the cheer on page 392 several times, with lots of energy and enthusiasm. Invite children to join you in reciting the cheer when they feel ready. Encourage them to find any new X/x and Ex/ex words in the cheer. Again, add these words to your list.

- Don't let your exploration of the letter X/x end with the story! Display your list of words in a place where children can easily see it. During the rest of the day or week, children can add new X/x and Ex/ex words that they encounter in other books, on signs, on food labels, and so on.

Today, X-ray Fish feels extra special.
It is his birthday!
X-ray Fish is expecting friends for a party.

The party is extremely fun.
Everyone plays pin-the-tail-
on-the-seahorse and other
exciting games.

At last, it is time for X-ray Fish
to open his gifts.
He knows exactly what he wants—
a xylophone!

X-ray Fish has x-ray vision.
He uses it to examine each gift
before he opens it.
Angelfish gives X-ray Fish a present.
Is it a xylophone?

No, but it is an excellent gift!
"Thanks for the ball!" exclaims X-ray Fish.

Next, Blowfish gives X-ray Fish a present.
Is it a xylophone?

No, but it is an excellent gift!
"Thanks for the boat!" exclaims X-ray Fish.

Then Tigerfish gives X-ray Fish a present.
Is it a xylophone?

No, but it is an excellent gift!
"Thanks for the teddy bear,"
exclaims X-ray Fish.

There is one present left to open.
The tag says, "To X-ray Fish from Mom.
XOXOXOXO." "All those X's mean
I love you," his mom explains.
Will this present be a xylophone?

It is a xylophone!
"Thank you for the excellent gift,"
says X-ray Fish. Then he unwraps it.
"It is exactly what I wanted!"

X-ray Fish plays "Happy Birthday"
on his new xylophone.
All his friends sing extra loud.

Then it is time to eat cake.
X-ray Fish is excited. With his x-ray vision,
he can see it is his favorite kind—
chocolate with seaweed filling!

Xx Cheer

X is for x-ray fish, swimming along.

X is for xylophone, to play a song.

What else starts with X? Not a whole lot.

But in tic-tac-toe, X marks the spot.

Hooray for X, big and small—

the most exceptional letter of all!

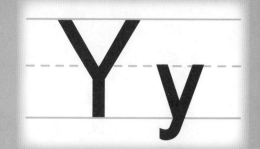
The Yak Who Yelled Yuck

By Carol Pugliano-Martin
Illustrated by Paul Harvey

Reading Tips

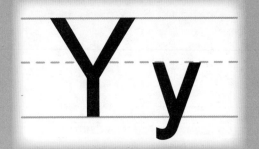

Here are some quick and fun ways to use this story to help children build important alphabet recognition skills.

- Ask children to find big Y and small y at the top of the previous page. Review the sound Y/y makes with children. Can they find three words in the title that begin with the letter Y/y? Read the title aloud, emphasizing the Y/y sound as appropriate.

- Ask children to point out words they hear or see that begin with Y/y. Explain that the story you are about to read includes many more words that begin with the letter Y/y. Can they help you find them?

- Read the story aloud once for pleasure and enjoy together the whimsical illustrations. Then reread the story, emphasizing the initial Y/y sound in the appropriate words. Ask children to listen closely for and identify all the words that start with Y/y. Point out these words in the text, and make a list of them.

- Write each of the words from your list on an unlined index card. Read each word on the cards aloud with children. On another reading of the story, children can match the words on the index cards with the words in the story.

- Read aloud the cheer on page 408 several times, with lots of energy and enthusiasm. Invite children to join you in reciting the cheer when they feel ready. Encourage them to find any new Y/y words in the cheer. Again, add these words to your list.

- Don't let your exploration of the letter Y/y end with the story! Display your list of words in a place where children can easily see it. During the rest of the day or week, children can add new Y/y words that they encounter in other books, on signs, on food labels, and so on.

There once was a young yak
who hated trying new foods.

One day, the young yak's father
gave her a yellow banana.

"YUCK!" yelled the yak without
even taking a bite.
The yak tossed the yellow banana
into her neighbor's yard.

The young yak's father
gave her some yogurt.

"YUCK!" yelled the yak.
She tossed the yogurt
into her neighbor's yard.

The young yak's father
gave her a yam.

"YUCK!" yelled the yak.
She tossed the yam into her neighbor's yard.

A wise old yak lived next door
to the young yak.
He was in his yard playing with his yo-yo.

The yam hit the wise old yak
right in the head!
"YIKES!" yelled the wise old yak.

"YOO-HOO, young yak!"
the wise old yak yelled over the fence.
"Yes?" said the young yak.
"You should taste things before you yell yuck,"
said the wise old yak.

The young yak leaped over the fence into her neighbor's yard.

She tasted the yellow banana,
the yogurt, and the yam.
"YOWEEE!" said the young yak.
"These are yummy!"

And now she's the yak who yells,
"YUM!"

Yy Cheer

Y is for yo-yo, Y is for yak.

Y is for a yummy yogurt snack.

Y is for yarn, yes, yard, and young.

Y is for yam and a bright yellow sun.

Hooray for big Y, small y, too—

the letter that makes you want to yell

"YAHOO!"

AlphaTales

Zz

Zack the Lazy Zebra

By Wendy Cheyette Lewison

Illustrated by Clive Scruton

Here are some quick and fun ways to use this story to help children build important alphabet recognition skills.

- Ask children to find big Z and small z at the top of the previous page. Review the Z/z sound with children. Can they find two words in the title that begin with the letter Z/z? Read the title aloud, emphasizing the Z/z sound as appropriate.

- Ask children to point out words they hear or see that begin with Z/z. Explain that the story you are about to read includes many more words that begin with the letter Z/z. Can they help you find them?

- Read the story aloud once for pleasure and enjoy together the whimsical illustrations. Then reread the story, emphasizing the initial Z/z sound in the appropriate words. Ask children to listen closely for and identify all the words that start with Z/z. Point out these words in the text, and make a list of them.

- Write each of the words from your list on an unlined index card. Read each word on the cards aloud with children. On another reading of the story, children can match the words on the index cards with the words in the story.

- Read aloud the cheer on page 424 several times, with lots of energy and enthusiasm. Invite children to join you in reciting the cheer when they feel ready. Encourage them to find any new Z/z words in the cheer. Again, add these words to your list.

- Don't let your exploration of the letter Z/z end with the story! Display your list of words in a place where children can easily see it. During the rest of the day or week, children can add new Z/z words that they encounter in other books, on signs, on food labels, and so on.

Zack the Zebra lives at the zoo.
All day long, what does Zack do?

Zz-zz-zz

The zookeepers bring a zebra snack.
But it doesn't wake up Zack.
Zack has no zest.
He wants to rest.

Zz-zz-zz

They zap Zack
with a garden hose.

They bang a drum.
They tickle his nose.

Zack's eyes stay closed.
He wants to doze.

Zz-zz-zz

They try a zillion zany tricks.

They hop around on pogo sticks.

Zack thinks their tricks are boring.
He goes on snoring.

Zz-zz-zz

Look! Here comes Zed,
a zebra with zing!

He zooms and zigzags
around everything.

Will Zed make Zack
wake up and leap?

No!
Now two zebras
want to sleep!

Zz-zz-zz
Zz-zz-zz

At last, the zookeepers
give up their schemes.
They wish Zack and Zed
sweet zebra dreams.

Zz-zz-zz
Zz-zz-zz

Zz Cheer

Z is for zebra, Z is for zoo.

Z is for zucchini and ziti, too.

Z is for zipper, Z is for zap.

Z is for zzzzzzz when you nap.

Hooray for Z, big and small—

the zippiest, zaniest letter of all!